FORMS OF GOVERNMENT: NEED TO KNOW

MONARCHY

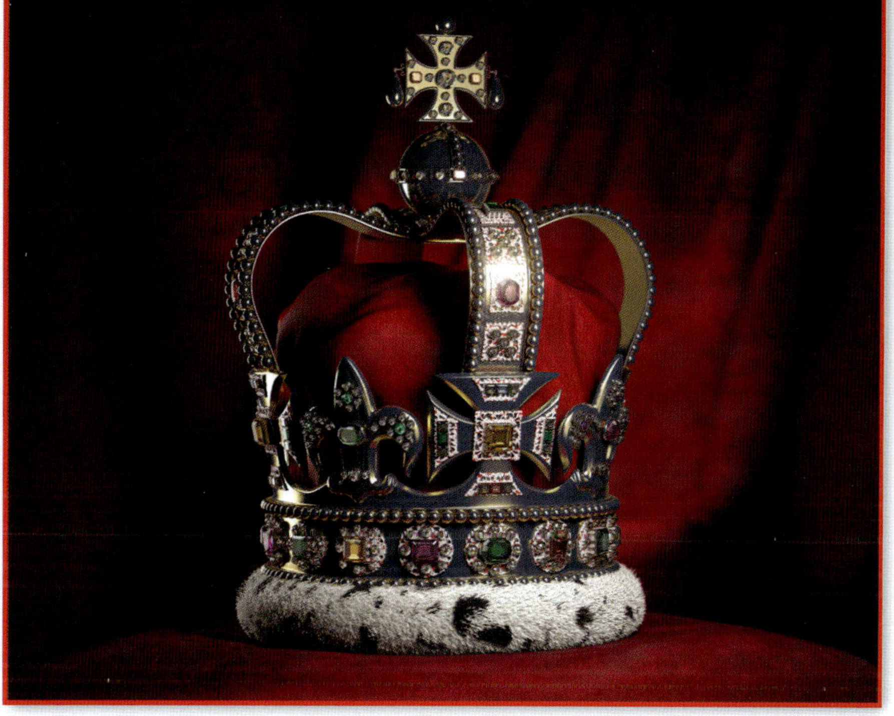

by D. R. Faust

Consultant: Caitlin Krieck, Social Studies Teacher and Instructional Coach, The Lab School of Washington

SilverTip Books, an imprint of Bearport Publishing by FlutterBee

Credits
Cover and title page, © Maxx-Studio/Shutterstock; 3, © PeskyMonkey/Shutterstock; 5, © Bettmann/Getty Images; 7, © Historical Picture Archive/Getty Images; 9, © TT News Agency/Alamy Stock Photo; 11, © D and S Photography Archives/Alamy Stock Photo; 13, © Maximum Exposure PR/Shutterstock; 15, © IanDagnall Computing/Alamy Stock Photo; 17, © Public Domain/Wikimedia Commons; 19, © walencienne/iStock; 21, © PA Images/Alamy Stock Photo; 23, © Tommy Muric/Shutterstock; 25, © duncan1890/iStock; 27, © Anadolu/Getty Images.

Bearport Publishing Company Product Development Team
Kayla Eggert, Theresa Emminizer, Kim Jones, Allison Juda, Cole Nelson, Naomi Reich, Steve Scheluchin, Tiana Tran

Statement on Usage of Generative Artificial Intelligence
Bearport Publishing remains committed to publishing high-quality nonfiction books. Therefore, we restrict the use of generative AI to ensure accuracy of all text and visual components pertaining to a book's subject. See BearportPublishing.com for details.

A Note on Colorization
Some of the historic photos in this book have been colorized to help readers have a more meaningful and rich experience. The color results are not intended to depict actual historical detail.

Library of Congress Cataloging-in-Publication Data is available at www.loc.gov or upon request from the publisher.

ISBN: 979-8-89577-637-7 (hardcover)
ISBN: 979-8-89577-791-6 (paperback)
ISBN: 979-8-89577-725-1 (ebook)

For more information, write to Bearport Publishing, 3500 American Blvd W, Suite 150, Bloomington, MN 55431. Printed in the United States of America.

Contents

Long Live the Queen

What is it like to be king or queen? You might picture huge castles and fancy clothes. But those are just a small part of being royal. Kings and queens are also leaders. They rule over governments called monarchies.

The head of a monarchy is called a monarch. The word comes from ancient Greek. It means one ruler.

I Rule!

Monarchies are led by one ruler. This person is the head of the whole government. There are two main kinds of monarchies. The first has no end to the monarch's power. They can do anything they want. The other has limits for what the ruler can do.

Leaders are called different things in different monarchies. They can be kings or queens. But some are called emperors or sultans.

How to Become a Ruler

How do people become monarchs? The role is usually passed on through a family. A monarch's child often becomes the new ruler. Some monarchs do not have children. Then, the next closest family member takes over.

Sometimes, the same family rules for a long time. This is called a **dynasty**.

The royal family of Sweden

There are also other ways monarchs come to power. A few are **elected** by a small group of powerful people. Others force their way in. They take over the government. Then, they kick out the monarch in power. They put themselves on the throne.

The Holy Roman Empire was a monarchy in Europe. It lasted for about a thousand years. The emperor was chosen by the pope and a council of electors.

Absolute Power

When one ruler has total control, it is an absolute monarchy. This monarch may have people who give them advice. But they do not have to take it. This ruler makes all the laws. They have the final say in everything the government does.

A ruler with full control is also called an **autocrat**. This title comes from a word meaning ruling by itself.

Mswati III of Eswatini is an absolute monarch.

Some absolute monarchs say their power comes from a god or gods. This is called the **divine** right. The idea helps keep these leaders in power. Few people question what they say. For them, it would be like going against a god.

Emperors in China said their power was a **mandate** of heaven. This meant a god or divine force selected them to rule.

King Louis XIV of France said he had a divine right to rule.

Limited Monarchy

Some monarchs have less control. This happens in a constitutional (*kaan*-stuh-TOO-shuh-nuhl) monarchy. This is also called a limited monarchy. The ruler is still the head of the government. But there are rules about what the monarch can and cannot do. These rules are set up by a **constitution**.

Many forms of government have constitutions. These are rules about how the government will run. They list what each part of the government can and cannot do.

CONSTITUTION
L'UNION FAIT LA FORCE
DE LA BELGIQUE.

Often, the monarch cannot make laws in a limited monarchy. This job is given to elected **officials**. The people vote for their lawmakers. Sometimes, the monarch can block a law. This is called a **veto**. But the ruler has very little other power.

The United Kingdom has a limited monarchy. It always has a king or queen. But a separate group makes the laws. Members of this group are picked by the people.

The Palace of Westminster

A National Symbol

Most monarchs today are part of limited monarchies. Their roles are mostly **ceremonial**. They are symbols of their countries. This means they often take part in celebrations. And they may visit other countries to meet with world leaders. But they do not have real power.

Modern Japan has a limited monarchy. The royal family is a symbol for the country. But a group called the National Diet makes the laws.

King Charles III of the United Kingdom holds many ceremonies.

Monarchs Through Time

This is a very old form of government. Some of the first monarchies were found in the Middle East. They spread from there. Egypt and India soon had monarchies, too. Monarchies boomed in the Middle Ages. They popped up all across Europe and Asia.

One of the oldest recorded monarchs was from ancient Egypt. This king was named Narmer. Historians believe Narmer ruled around 3100 BCE.

King Narmer of ancient Egypt

Some rulers in the Middle Ages gave land to **nobles**. These were a bit like lesser kings. They ruled over smaller parts of the monarch's lands. This helped the monarchs stay in power. But over time, governments changed. Some became limited monarchies. Others shifted to entirely new governments.

What caused the shift in governments? Often, it was what the people wanted. They did not want to be under the control of nobles and monarchs. They wanted more of a say for themselves.

Ego Willms cognoie Bastard' Rex Anglie do t
ccedo tibi Nepoti meo Alano Britannie comiti
t heredibs tuis inppetm omes villas t tras que

Modern Monarchs

There are far fewer monarchies than there once were. But there are still some around today. Many monarchs in power now rule differently than leaders of the past. They have changed with the times. And they will likely continue to do so.

There are more than 40 national governments that still have monarchies. Many are limited. But more than 10 percent of monarchies are absolute.

King Salman became the absolute monarch of Saudi Arabia in 2015.

Forms of Monarchy

Monarchies can be absolute or limited. Their rulers have different powers.

	Absolute Monarchy	Limited Monarchy
Definition	A form of government where a single royal leader holds total power	A form of government where a royal leader holds limited powers as laid out in a constitution
Lawmaking Power	The monarch may make any law they wish	Laws are made by elected officials rather than the monarch
Monarchs and Other Countries	The monarch can make treaties or go to war with other countries	The monarch may meet with other leaders but cannot make decisions
Examples	Saudi Arabia	The United Kingdom

SilverTips for SUCCESS

★SilverTips for REVIEW

Review what you've learned. Use the text to help you.

Define key terms

absolute monarchy
ceremonial
constitutional monarchy
dynasty
monarch

Check for understanding

What are the different ways monarchs can come to power?

Explain the key differences between an absolute monarchy and a limited monarchy.

Describe one way the role of monarchs has changed throughout history.

Think deeper

How would your life be different if the form of government in your city, state, or nation changed?

★SilverTips for TAKING TESTS

- **Make a study plan.** Ask your teacher what the test is going to cover. Then, set aside time to study a little bit every day.
- **Read all the questions carefully.** Be sure you know what is being asked.
- **Skip any questions** you don't know how to answer right away. Mark them and come back later if you have time.

Glossary

autocrat a person who rules with total power

ceremonial for show and without real power or influence

constitution a document with the basic laws and principles for governing

divine related to or coming from a god or gods

dynasty a group of rulers from the same family

elected selected by vote for an office, position, or membership

mandate an official order or command

nobles people who are members of the highest class in some societies

officials people who hold an office or important position

veto the power of a person to decide that something will not be approved

Read More

Davis, Jane R. *Ten Terrible Kings and Queens (History's Very Worst)*. Buffalo, NY: Gareth Stevens Publishing, 2026.

Hudak, Heather C. *Lost Kings and Kingdoms (History Raiders)*. New York: Crabtree Publishing Company, 2022.

Kim, Carol. *The Secret Lives of Pharaohs (Secrets of Ancient Civilizations)*. North Mankato, MN: Capstone Press, 2025.

Learn More Online

1. Go to **FactSurfer.com** or scan the QR code below.
2. Enter "**Monarchy**" into the search box.
3. Click on the cover of this book to see a list of websites.

Index

About the Author

D. R. Faust is a freelance writer of fiction and nonfiction. They live in Queens, NY.